Secrets of a Midwest Morel Mushroom Hunter

By James Sterling

PREFACE

Greetings… My name is James, I live in the Midwest and I have been hunting and gathering morel mushrooms for over twenty years. In those years I have gathered thousands of morel mushrooms and learned many things during my time in the great Outdoors. I would like to pass this information on to you, plus give you some tips at the end that no one else will tell you! I hope this text informs you and your descendants and helps carry on this great tradition. Please remember to always be safe out there – now let the hunt begin!

WHERE TO FIND MORELS

There is a magical event that occurs across the U.S. every spring-time but only for a short time. The first thing every mushroom hunter should know is that morel mushrooms grow where they please and only where they please. There are indeed some general areas that will always produce, and in this book we will explore how to find these locations in the woods of North America, specifically in the Midwest.

We will look at which types of trees, plants, soils, elevations, air temps, moisture levels, grade of slopes, and facing of hill surfaces, to name a few, that will help you land your best search results. We will discuss the hazards involved with traversing potentially treacherous locations, general tips and tricks, what equipment you should carry to hunt morels safely, and some of my secret methods for obtaining morels that I have learned from my long years in the woods of North America; secrets that I have not told a living soul before the writing of this text.

TYPES OF MORELS

Now for the star of the show. It is vitally important to note that true morels are completely hollow inside – any solid stem morels are false and known to be poisonous. Any species of morel you collect should not be eaten raw; true morels must be cooked thoroughly to be safe for human consumption.

The main morels found in the Midwest and Eastern North America are the black morel, the yellow morel, and the grey morel.

Morchella elata

Black Morel

Morchella elata, or the black morel, is a family of true morels generally found first in the season before the yellows and greys. They are the most likely to be found in large patches.

Sub-species by region:
Eastern North America

Morchella angusticeps

Morchella septentrionalis

Western North America

Morchella brunnea

Morchella capitata

Morchella importuna

Morchella septimelata

Morchella sextelata

Morchella snyderi

Morchella tomentosa

Morchella esculenta

Yellow Morel

Morchella esculenta, or the yellow morel, is a family of true morels that appear yellow in color and across the Midwest are known as the main event of the mushroom season. These appear latest in the season, usually scattered, but sometimes found in banana-like clusters. These can grow quite large if not harvested.

Gray Morel

The Midwestern Gray Morel is also now considered part of the *morchella esculenta* family and are actually the early form of the characteristic yellow morel. Early in the spring they certainly stand out and look like a different species than the yellows, as you can see in the image below.

Half – Free Morel

The half- free morel is a species of true morel that is easily spotted due to its difference in appearance to the yellow, gray, and black morels. This species can be easily confused so make sure your finds have hollow centers! If the center is not hollow, it is not a true morel that is edible.

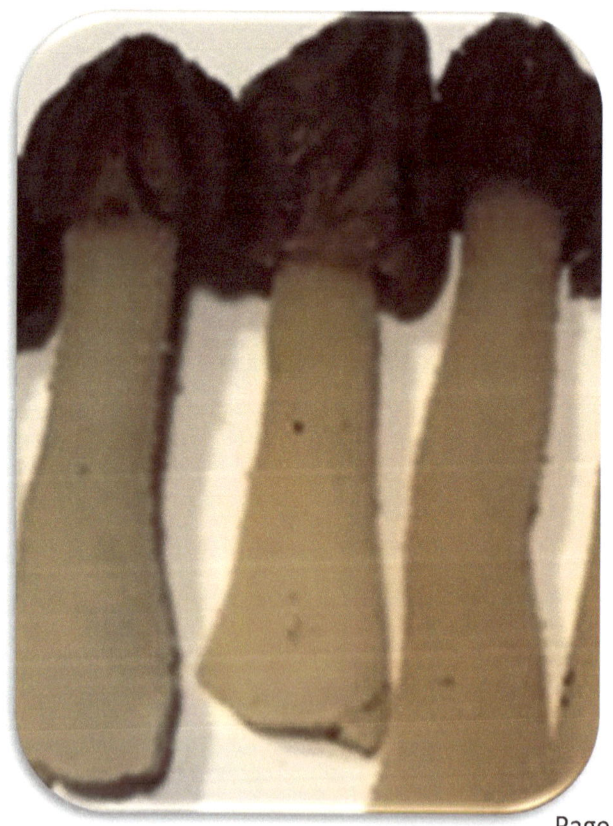

Species and Location:

Morchella punctipes (Eastern North America)

Morchella populiphila (Western North America)

Morchella semilibera (Europe)

TREES, HILLS, & PLANTS...OH MY!

There are many factors that will help you find these delicious fungi. Namely, the trees they grow near and under; where to look on hills, hillsides, and slopes; and which plants will help guide you to your target.

First, we will study the trees species that seem to produce the best results in the woods and forests of the Midwestern United States of America.

American Elm (*ulmus americana*)

The single most important species you can look for in the woods of midwestern and eastern America is the American Elm tree, or species *ulmus americana*. All types of morels described in this book are noted to appear in large quantities and sizes around this tree species.

The American elm is a large deciduous tree that if allowed to grow for its normal lifespan, several hundred years, grows over one hundred and forty feet tall with a large spread open canopy that dominates the forest ceiling wherever it grows.

The majority of mature American Elm trees in the United States were inflicted by Dutch Elm Disease starting in 1928 when a shipment of logs carrying several species of elm bark beetles arrived via the Netherlands for use in furniture. These beetles carried and spread the fungus that causes Dutch Elm disease and ravaged the native elm populations of North America for the next several decades. Between 1930 and 1989, over 75% of the estimated 77 million elm trees in North America were lost due to this disease.

An elm tree is notable for its shaggy loss of bark when it is nearing and after death of the tree. To identify this, several factors come into play. One sign you will look for is if you look at the main trunk of the tree underneath the bark that has stripped away, you will see squiggly lines reminiscent of insects burrowing underground. Often you will walk upon and notice the tree simply due to its loss of bark. Generally, at least in the Midwest, the bark upon falling away has the outer bark layer that falls off – and nearing complete death of the tree there will be a thin red layer of material between the outer bark and the main trunk.

It cannot be stressed enough how important this is to learn if you wish to find morels of any decent amount and mass. Mycelium grow under the soil looking for nutrients through a root structure, as it is further explained in other sections of this text, and once enough nutrients are found, the roots "bloom" and rise above the soil in the form of the characteristic morel sponge shape to release their spores. In doing so, the species will germinate and continue to survive. One reason that is believed that morels are so prevalent around elm trees has to do with their massive die-offs wherever DED lingers or any number of other tree disease species ravage the area – releasing tons of nutrients into the soil from the decaying plant matter of the rotting tree structure from the very roots to the ends of the branches.

The most noted abundances of morels surrounding this species occur around elm species near to death or very shortly after death – when the bark is just beginning to crack and strip away and you have that red lining we mentioned earlier peeking through.

Fortunately, for morel mushroom hunters across North America and the elm and morel species' themselves, there is hope for the American elm and all elm species native to this continent. As of 2005, scientists are currently cultivating 19 disease resistant elm strains and experimenting with mixing the different elm species together to create hybrids that will resist Dutch elm disease and other harmful tree diseases.

White Ash/American Ash
(*fraxinus americana*)

The second most active producer of morel prevalence in the Midwest is the White Ash tree, or species *fraxinus americana*. Every form of morel has been detected in the immediate area surrounding this species.

The most obvious characteristics of this tree is the tree structure itself and the pattern of its bark. White ash trees tend to grow to sizes of around 90 feet and live for approximately 70 years if not killed off or chopped down during its lifetime.

This species is very notable during autumn for its primarily red colors with some turning bright orange as is the case of deciduous trees turning color and then losing their leaves during the winter season in North America. Other ash species tend to turn more of a yellow hue.

Unfortunately, as with the American elm, this tree species is being threatened with widespread destruction. This time, however, it is not a disease that threatens the white ash, but an insect. The Emerald ash borer is an invasive species of green beetle from Asia and currently threatens over 7.5 billion ash trees in central and eastern North America alone. Comparatively, only 200 million elm trees were affected by Dutch elm disease.

White Ash Tree

American Sycamore (Platanus occidentalis)

The American sycamore is best known for its distinct white papery bark as you travel up the trunk of the tree and for their immense size. This tree often grows up around 130 feet tall and has been known to grow much taller in rare cases. The bark often starts out brown and turns white the farther up you go. It is also known for its white papery bark appearing to be in a state of flaking away from the trunk.

This is another specimen around which morels are often found and has been confirmed in recent years – although not nearly as commonly as with the elm or ash noted above.

Sycamore

Various other species

It has been, and continues to be, reported that morels have been found around and under the shade of pine trees, in great quantities in old decaying apple orchards, and even around tulip trees in the Midwest. The author of this text has been unable to verify these reports. As an additional caution concerning old apple orchards, if the site still contains remnants of the pesticide lead arsenate, dangerous levels of lead and arsenic have been discovered.

Burn Sites

Curiously, morels appear in great abundance the year after a forest fire burns a section of the forest. This is suspected to be due to the great release of nutrients from all the vegetation, now rotting due to being killed off by the fire. Again, it should be noted that the mycelium, which creates the morels, lives off of nutrients seeping into the soil.   These mycelium networks grow under the soil, and often survive the fire ravaging the forest above.

Since forest fires generally occur more towards the West and Northwest in the United States, this has not been observed in the Midwest during springtime. A popular place to search in that case would be not only naturally caused forest fires, such as those caused by lightning sparking dry foliage, but also human caused burns – usually created as wind breaks or other types of forest management.

Black morels, Morchella elata, are known to prefer sites that have been burned previously, and disturbed soils in general.

Hills, Hill-sides, and Slopes

In early spring, morels start growing when the soil reaches warmer temperatures, after the long cold of winter. Naturally, hill-sides facing to the south receive more sunlight than those facing other cardinal directions. This is the first place you should look in the Spring. Notedly, even flat land at first does not receive as much sunlight and in return, warmth, as south facing hillsides.

If you want to get the leg up on other morel mushroom hunters and gatherers, you should be looking at types of land in this order; South-facing hill-sides, hill-tops, east and west facing slopes, and finally north facing hill-sides which receive the least amount of sunlight in the Spring. This leads us to discuss the soil itself, which we will cover in the next chapter.

As stated in the beginning of this book, morels grow where they please, therefore I will refrain from stating what types of hill-sides are best to look around. Morels have been found on gently sloping land just as well as on sharp embankments or even in areas flat and devoid of any elevation.

SOIL CONDITIONS

Soil Temperatures

You read that correctly, soil conditions are extremely important in determining where and when morels will be found.

Namely, the most important factor here will be soil temperatures, as in where does the sun hit the ground first and for the longest time. A good resource to study leading up to the season and a handy trick is to follow the farmers! Farmers in the Midwest heavily track soil temperatures to determine when to plant their crops, their main source of money. Therefore, we use the same tools as they do – there are many websites online which track soil temperatures in the United States. These websites often have private owners and operators and thusly we will just discuss what to search for. Using any search engine, searching the terms "soil temperatures" "spring" "planting crops" "Midwest" should get you a few hundred results at least. Any of the big-name sites that come up in your search will have maps of soil temperatures for your perusal – many are public, and are viewed for no charge, for farming and scientific reasons.

Let us get into specifics on what you are actually looking for while using these maps. The consensus among those searching for morels is that they generally appear once your soil temps reach an average of at least 45 to 50 degrees Fahrenheit. What is most important is that the soil is warm enough to remain above freezing over night and since soil loses some temperature during the cooler night time hours, this must be heavily considered. In general, let your day time air temperatures hit 60 to 65 degrees Fahrenheit and as long as your nights are not dropping below freezing, you should be golden.

Later in the season, things really start kicking off when you enter the range of the 70s Fahrenheit. Morels love warmth but also cool, humid air for the moisture to absorb and grow. The best results are shown year after year to be pulled from areas experiencing air temperatures in the 70s during the day and 50s during the night.

It is often said that you see morels starting to appear around the same time as you see dandelions blooming in your yard

or when the lilac bushes start blooming –
this is all because of the soil heating up to a
temperature you are looking for to discover
morels.

Soil Types

Morels are observed to enjoy growing in loose, sandy soils where they have room to breathe and grow. Signs to look out for, therefore, are sandy, loamy soils where the ground is darker earth but still of a sandy texture if you put it between your fingers. The same can be said for crops to grow – they need room to spread their roots but also have moisture from rain able to seep into the soil.

Morels (and plant-life in general) do not like and do not grow in clay or soil heavily featuring clay. This is due to the very low oxygen content in clay and how tight the material is in such a soil. This is one reason it is used to make ceramic objects; generally, you want such products to hold together and not leak. Clay is heavily used in industrial activities and a majority of the Earth's population still live in dwellings made with clay- rich materials such as brick and cement. Historically, clay was predominately used for building as it was an abundant material readily available for use.

Soil Moisture

All fungal type species are mainly comprised of water. In cases where water is scarce, you will see less types and numbers of mushrooms. The heavy thunderstorms of Spring in the Midwest are a major reason why morels love this location and time of year, and grow in such numbers.

WILDLIFE AND OTHER HAZARDS

Wild animals should always be given a wide berth – some more than others. In this region of the United States, the most common large animal you will find is the white-tailed deer, known for its distinctive white furred tail that is usually the only part of the animal you see as it runs away. In many areas these animals are overpopulated and hunted for their venison. This leads to conditions where it is common in this region to actually drive into a small herd of them while they cross the road if you aren't careful. Most of the time these are harmless animals that just want to be left in peace – you will hear them running away from you in the woods far more often than you will see them.

Farther north towards Minnesota you will run into Moose, the largest deer species, and can be quite deadly if not left alone. Special care should be given if you happen upon a mother and her calf – leave the area immediately but do not cause a disturbance.

Not to be left out are the carnivores in some areas, usually found in the mountainous regions such as the Appalachian trail and the ranges in upper New York state. Carnivorous animals sometimes found wandering into the Midwest include the Black Bear, the Cougar, the Bobcat, the Timber Wolf, and the Badger. These sightings are very rare but it is always good to know what animals have the ability to be in your area, especially while in their natural habitat. When we are out in the woods and forests, we are in their natural home, not ours, and should be given the proper respect.

Smaller carnivores that are more populous and known to live in the Midwest are the Coyote, the Red Fox, the bird species such as owls, and the various snake species.

Other hazards include the terrain itself, the weather, chance of injury - especially if you are not carrying the proper safety items and a communication device such as a cell phone.

It should be noted that the Midwest is notorious for having large populations of deer ticks. Ticks carry Lyme disease and must be avoided at all costs. A quick check of your hair and limbs after you exit the woods is highly recommended. Take care not to bring any back for your pets as well.

GLORY OF THE WALKING STICK

One of your largest and most important tools will be to carry a walking stick, or staff, with you while walking in wooded areas. There are individuals who fashion their own creations complete with painted, carved, and stained options and sell them online. Or you may just simply look around on the forest floor and find your own sturdy branch, normally 5 or 6 feet long. You can either take it home and shave it down to a decent size with no protrusions to catch your hand on or you might just use it as you found it. Make sure it is sturdy and will not break easily before you put any weight on the wood.

A good source to look for is a recently fallen tree that has died but still has branches attached. This sometimes gives you a less rotten length of wood to decrease your chances of it breaking.

The advantages to having this tool are numerous. Besides the obvious boon to having something to lean on, there are side benefits to a walking stick. First of all, what better way to move leaves around on the forest floor without straining your back. This makes it easier to see if there are any morels hiding in your vicinity. Your walking stick will become an extension of yourself as you continue mushroom hunting.

Another advantage is that while strolling through a particularly thick briar patch or area containing thorny plants and trees, you can use your walking stick to hold back the dangerous foliage and allow yourself to pass under or around a prickly thicket.

It is unlikely that you would run into any animal or person that would harm you in the forest, but it is also nice to have that extra protection if only for your peace of mind.

A more minor advantage to having a walking stick is that if you are carrying extra clothes or a bag for holding your finds, you can hang these items on your stick and lighten your load. It is helpful to make a small notch in one end so your item will stay put without getting lost in the trees and undergrowth.

Example of a walking stick

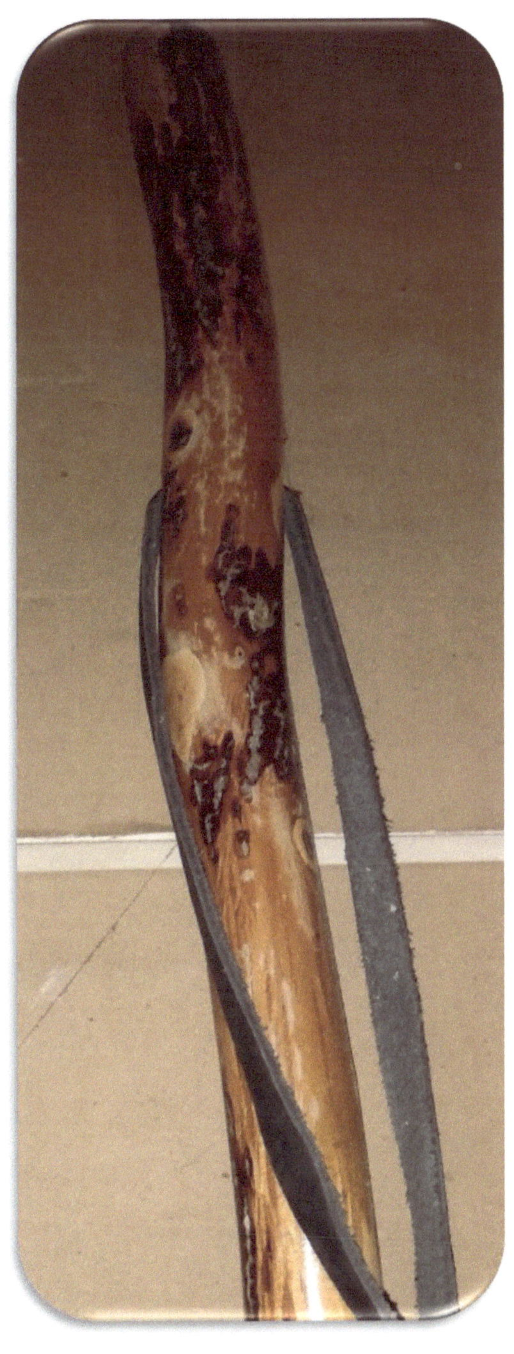

THE MIND OF THE MOREL

There are many curiosities attached to this camouflaged morsel. Some days you will find that perfect tree or section of woods where everything is just what you should need to have buckets of morels. And some days you will find just that. But on some days, you will also have strange encounters with morels.

The morel, as far as we are aware, is not a sentient species. However, scientists have detected intelligence in many creatures that we do not consider sentient, such as elephants and dolphins. Other lifeforms such as plants and fungi do not seem to show conscious thought but sometimes you will swear that they do after many hours in a forest. That creak of boughs; that sway of a branch catching your eye; that sound of leaves moving – all can lead your mind to ponder if that really was a trick of the wind.

Plants and fungi, however, do show evidence of chemical based reactions. One example would be the Venus fly trap knowing when an insect has landed in its midst. Another would be running into a patch of stinging nettles – you will know when you have done so. These and other defense mechanisms show that some plants and fungi have a sort of awareness of their surroundings, at least when in contact with a danger such as a deer coming along to chew their leaves. You can certainly see the evolution of a plant's defense mechanism when you run into its thorns; or a fungus' defense mechanism of being poisonous when ingested. Every living thing tries its best to exist and keep on existing and some must get creative to do so.

You will notice the strange behavior mentioned above with morels by the strange locations you stumble upon them. They have been known to pop up around railroad tracks, along pathways, in people's gardens, even underwater in an area that floods off and on. You expect to find them in a patch but you may find one in an area and no others for quite some time. Persistence is key to gathering morels.

WEATHER

We briefly covered certain dangerous weather conditions in the chapter about hazards – but there are many factors to weather you need to consider. Above all, yes, the weather can be hazardous and even deadly at times. It is vital that you check the weather for the area you will be in as phenomenon such as severe thunderstorms do occur. It is more dangerous to be out among tall trees that act as lightning rods than it is to be safe at home. If lightning strikes a tree you are under at the time, there is a very good chance you will be hit by the blast going through the tree into the ground around you.

The Midwest is notorious for other weather emergencies such as flash floods and tornadoes. We are on the eastern end of what meteorologists call "Tornado Alley." One should not discount this fact, as a storm can blow in much faster than the time it would take you to exit the area. There have been many cases where a storm spawned not only one tornado, or funnel cloud, but many that strike the entire region. As the planet heats up, whether from human caused climate change or from natural processes, a phenomenon known as a derecho is becoming much more common. A derecho is a very fast-moving wind storm than can sweep through a state, causing widespread wind damage and resulting power outages. They can be hundreds of miles long and move in a large line, or front, and sweep through a distance of hundreds of miles wide. The point is, weather such as this can rush in and catch you unawares unless you are vigilant and watch your local weather before you leave your home.

Flash floods are slightly less common but as much or even more dangerous. A particularly strong thunderstorm can douse an area that is already saturated from previous storms. If the ground is unable to absorb the excess water, it has to go somewhere. The end result is creeks and rivers break their banks and rise in a large, fast- moving deadly event. If you see a creek or river swollen and even just barely covering a road, do not walk or drive through it. Go around it if you can, because you never know when a bridge will suddenly give out or a strong current will sweep your vehicle or person entirely off the road or path. If you see a good chance of strong storms that day, it would be wise to wait it out or move your hunt to another day.

Aside from the dangers of weather emergencies, there are other factors to consider in weather's relation to the growth of morels. The best time to find a new germination of morels and other fungi is to go out the day after an overnight soaking rain. This provides the moisture they need to grow in abundance and you will notice they definitely take advantage of these rain events.

On the flip side, a long stretch of dry weather is very much what morels despise. If you are in the woods and the undergrowth is audibly crunchy and the soil is hard to the touch, this does not bode well for the spawning of morels. You may consider waiting for a few rainy days before heading back to that area.

An area devoid of moisture and humidity in general will not produce any large amounts of what you seek. Plan your days out according to your local weather forecast.

If you do happen to get caught in a severe thunderstorm, it is not wise to be around a tall structure such as a large tree or to be the tallest thing in a stretch of flat land. This is why you hear of so many near miss lightning strikes on golf courses. You may wish to hunker down away from such areas and wait the storm out or retreat to your vehicle for safety.

OTHER SECRETS & TIPS

Now I will give you some short advice to expediate your hunt for morels and also include a few pointers for common courtesy to the natural area and other hunters.

When traversing the woods looking for morels, always carry a mesh bag with you to hold your finds. This allows the spores from the morels you find to fall back to the ground as they should so that the species may continue to reproduce. You may even increase the odds for the next season by spreading those spores yourself!

If you are lucky enough to find the elusive morel, care should be given to how you pick it and remove it from the area. It is thought that the best way to pick a morel is to put your fingers together at the base of the mushroom and either use a pocketknife to remove it from the stem or pinch and remove it, giving care that you do not pull the root of the mushroom out as well. This gives the mycelium in the soil the best chance at not being harmed from the activity.

Quick Tips to Successful Hunts

This will be more of an informal, rapid-fire type section that you typically would not see in a book like this; however, I am including it for those instances where you are out in the wild and want some information quick about what to do and where to go.

After you enter a wooded area that you have permission to be in, stop and look at the trees around you. Use the Trees section to study the bark and tree crown patterns around you.

If you are looking for the elms, look for the bark stripping away from the tree. If you are looking for ash, look for the X pattern in the bark and the high crown of the tree. If you are looking for sycamore, look for a large, thick trunk that tapers into usually all white flakey bark by the time you get to the lower branches.

Look for any dead trees in general, fungi love rotting wood and it certainly increases your odds. Study the area around the rotting wood, if you see other species of mushroom, Do Not Touch them as they could be deadly poisonous.

However, it speaks to the conditions of the area that if one species of fungus can survive, that generally means morels can as well.

As stated previously, fungi thrive on moisture so look for moist soil. If the soil is too dry, you may want to wait for an overnight rain or thunderstorm. Morels also like soil disturbances, so those thunderstorms may just kick up a large fruiting of morels the next day.

Look alongside creeks and any other notedly wet areas – if you can find the right trees and add in that moisture from the water, that doubles your odds.

If you notice any trees that look split open but are still alive, or that look slightly charred, they may have been hit by lightning during the last thunderstorm. Search the surrounding area thoroughly.

Look down at the undergrowth, if you see several-inch-high umbrella plants, maybe at the flowering stage; or the early stages of the normal woodland plant life in your area, this is a good sign that you are out during the right time of year. Watch out for any vines or thick bushes, there is a good chance they have thorns and getting caught up in those is not pleasant for your clothes or your skin.

Before even entering the woods, look for lilacs blooming and yards full of yellow dandelions – this means the soil is warmed up enough to support morels.

Once the air temps in your area settle into the constant 80s and 90s, you have missed your window – the soil is now too warm to support morels and all you may find is any lingering on north facing hillsides or just the decaying remains of the morels that have already fruited.

Take care to do the research on your area to spot wooded areas that are open for public use and not private property. Use care when considering forest preserves and reserves which are usually monitored to protect the flora and fauna inside. Never pick or remove any item that is restricted in that location. Hunting for morels is indeed a fun activity or hobby but it is not to be done illegally – or you may find yourself behind bars and burdened with a large fine. Always ask for permission from the local land owner if that area is private property – many of them may even let you keep the hauls or split them with you. Some land owners are unable to hunt for morels themselves and are happy to make a deal with you or even pay you in return for morels you may find. The bottom line here is Do Not Trespass on private property for any reason.

What to Bring Along

-Mesh bag

-Water

-Trail snacks

-Toiletries

-Cell phone with full battery

-Portable battery for cell recharge (optional)

-Appropriate attire

-Light jacket

-Walking stick

-Your wits and the knowledge provided to you by this text

-Compass (optional)

-Umbrella (optional)

-Tick/Insect repellant (optional)

THE LEGACY

Why must mushroom hunting be
preserved?

As the human world turns more and more electronic in nature, it is important to remember what brought us to this point. While morels may not be a primary crop or food source, it remains vitally important that this legacy remain intact for many, many reasons.

Hunting morels is not just about the finding and gathering, those are the end results. The journey to get to that point is just as important. As they say, stop and smell the wild roses – while there are still wild roses to smell.

As important as morels are to us today, they were even more important to the ancient hunter-gatherers of North America. Combined with planting crops, gathering wild foliage, fishing, and hunting game, mushrooms provided the diet that was necessary to help us evolve into the species we are today. Like them or not, they are a part of us.

Despite the historical reasons, one that cannot be ignored is how physical and thrilling the search for them can sometimes be – once you have scaled hills for hours on end and walked long trails in search of these precious morsels, you begin to understand that it takes a commitment to get out into the woods day after day; but one that pays off every time.

If we do not take care of our forests, this may become a lost practice and one less method we have for getting necessary exercise in the Spring months. Keep hunting those fungi, and your family, your doctor, even you will thank yourself.

In addition to the physically moving our muscles aspects of hunting morels are additional health benefits such as lowering our blood sugar levels, getting our eyes out of an electronic screen all day, preventing diabetes, assisting to prevent obesity, and even just balancing our mental states – giving ourselves a chance to relieve stress in a healthy manner.

The joy and wonders of nature itself must not be understated, it may take you a few trips outdoors but you will hopefully come to respect the beauty of being among so many forms of life while searching for one or more of our natural treasures. One that only exists in a visible state for a few weeks out of the entire year. We have an attachment to the natural world that is being lost day by day and if we aren't careful, we may entirely lose out on this privilege. Families may lose a vital tradition that has been passed down for unknown generations.

Fortunately, all the negatives described need not come to pass. We have the power to save our natural world, and in the process, ourselves.

Explore More with Books by Sterling

Thank you for reading Secrets of a Midwest Morel Mushroom Hunter! If you're passionate about wild mushroom foraging, outdoor adventure, or nature-inspired stories, there's more waiting for you. Visit booksbysterling.com to discover additional field guides, survival tips, and original fiction inspired by America's wild landscapes. Whether you're hunting morels or escaping into a thrilling novel, you'll find something worth exploring.

Text Copyright ©2021 James Sterling

Cover Art & Images ©2021 James Sterling

All Rights Reserved

No part of this publication may be reproduced, distributed, or

transmitted in any form or by any means, including photocopying,

recording, or other electronic or mechanical methods, or by any

information storage and retrieval system without the prior written

permission of the publisher, except in the case of very brief quotations

embodied in critical reviews and certain other noncommercial uses

permitted by copyright law.

www.ingramcontent.com/pod-product-compliance
Lightning Source LLC
Chambersburg PA
CBHW040229240726

48664CB00001B/64